HAL•LEONARD®
SAXOPHONE
PLAY-ALONG

AUDIO
ACCESS
INCLUDED

Speed • Pitch • Balance • Loop

VOL. 2

CONTENTS

E♭ Saxophones	B♭ Saxophones	Title
2	42	Cleo's Mood JUNIOR WALKER & THE ALL STARS
4	33	I Got a Woman RAY CHARLES
10	39	Pick Up the Pieces AVERAGE WHITE BAND
13	44	Respect ARETHA FRANKLIN
18	49	Shot Gun JUNIOR WALKER & THE ALL STARS
26	54	Soul Finger THE BAR-KAYS
23	56	Soul Serenade KING CURTIS
28	59	Unchain My Heart RAY CHARLES

To access audio visit:
www.halleonard.com/mylibrary
Enter Code
2666-9618-5472-7960

ISBN 978-1-4803-0001-9

HAL•LEONARD®
7777 W. BLUEMOUND RD. P.O. BOX 13819 MILWAUKEE, WI 53213

Visit Hal Leonard Online at
www.halleonard.com

Cleo's Mood

Words and Music by Autry DeWalt, Willie J. Woods and Harvey Fuqua

I Got a Woman

Words and Music by Ray Charles and Renald J. Richard

man. ___ I ___ got a wom-an ___ 'way __ o-ver

town _____ that's good to ___ me. ___ Whoa, _____

yeah. ___ Ah don't-cha know she's al - right.

Ah don't-cha know she's al - right. She's al - right, she's al -

right. Whoa, _____ yeah. _____

Oh, yeah. _____

9

Pick Up the Pieces

Words and Music by James Hamish Stuart, Alan Gorrie, Roger Ball, Robbie McIntosh, Owen McIntyre and Malcolm Duncan

Respect

Words and Music by Otis Redding

good times keep on try - in'. You're run -

in' out of fools, and I ain't lyin'.

'Spect when you come home, __ or you might

walk in and find out I'm gone. I got to have __

lit - tle re - spect.

Shot Gun

Words and Music by Autry DeWalt

Do the jerk, ba - by. ___   Do the jerk, now. ___

F7

Hey!

Sax solo:

Fl. ___

I said,

F7

shot - gun. ___

Shoot him 'fore he run, now.

Organ:

Do the jerk, ba - by. __

Do the jerk now. __ Hey! Put on __ your high- heeled shoes. __

Guitar:

mp

I said we're go - in' down here __ an' lis - ten to 'em play

the blues. We're gon - na dig po - ta. __ we're gon - na

Organ:

f

pick to - ma - tas __ I said shot - gun. __

Shoot him 'fore he run, now.

Do the jerk, ba - by. ___   Do the jerk, now. ___

Hey!   I said it's   twin - in' time. ___   I said it's

twin - in' time.   I said it's   twin - in' time.   Hey,

what did I say?   *Sax solo:*

Fl. ———

Fadeout

Soul Serenade

Words and Music by Curtis Ousley and Luther Dixon

Soul Finger

**Words and Music by Ben Cauley, Carl Cunningham, James Alexander,
Jimmy King, Phalon Jones and Ronnie Caldwell**

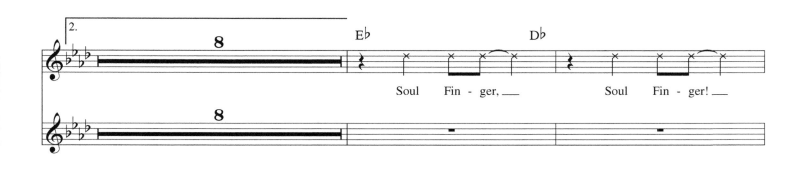

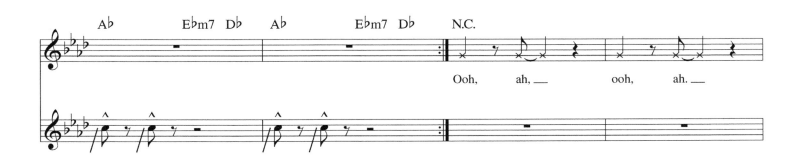

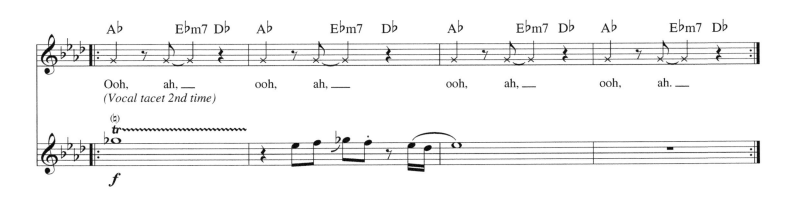

Unchain My Heart

Words and Music by Bobby Sharp and Teddy Powell

but you're let - tin' my love go to waste, ___ so un - chain ___
some fel - la tells me that you're not at home, ___ so un - chain ___

___ my heart, ___ oh please, ___ please set me free. ___
___ my heart, ___ oh please, ___ please set me free. ___

1. Un - chain my heart.

2. I'm un - der your spell ___

like a man in a trance, ___ but I know darn ___ well ___

that I don't stand a chance, ___ so un - chain my heart. ___

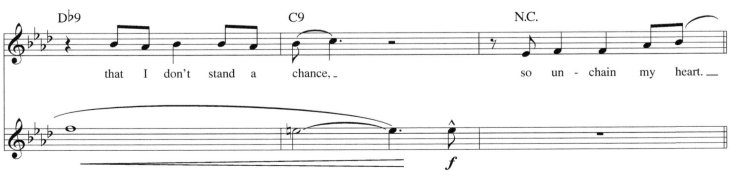

I Got a Woman

Words and Music by Ray Charles and Renald J. Richard

yes, __ she's a kind of __ friend in-

deed. _____ I got a wom-an _____ 'way o-ver

town _____ that's good to __ me. Oh, yeah. __

_____ She saves her lov - in' ear - ly in the

morn - ing just for me. ___ Oh, __ yeah. __

_____ She saves her lov - in' ear - ly in the

morn - ing   just for ___ me. _____   Oh, ___

yeah. ___   She saves her lov - in'   just for

me.   Yeah, _____ she _____ will love _____ me ___ so ten - der -

ly. ___   I ___ got a wom - an _____   'way _ o - ver

town _____   that's good to ___ me.   Oh, ___

yeah. ___

Solo:

Pick Up the Pieces

**Words and Music by James Hamish Stuart, Alan Gorrie, Roger Ball,
Robbie McIntosh, Owen McIntyre and Malcolm Duncan**

⊕ Coda

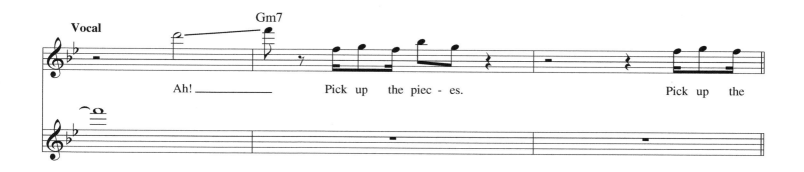

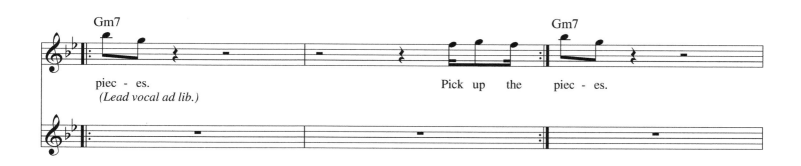

Cleo's Mood

Words and Music by Autry DeWalt, Willie J. Woods and Harvey Fuqua

Respect

Words and Music by Otis Redding

home, yeah. ___

Solo:

C#   h.t.

G#m

A7
Ooh, ___

A   G   A
___ your kiss is   sweet-er than hon-ey,   and guess what, ___

G   A   G
so ___ is my mon-ey.   All I want you to do for me   is give it to me

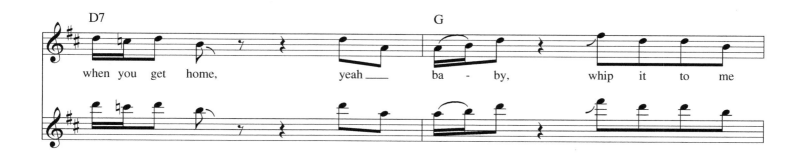

when you get home, yeah___ ba - by, whip it to me

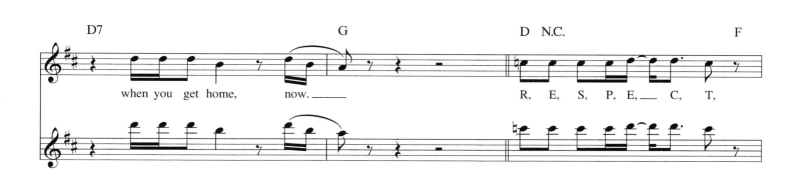

when you get home, now.___ R, E, S, P, E,___ C, T,

find out what it means_ to me. R, E, S, P, E,___ C, T,

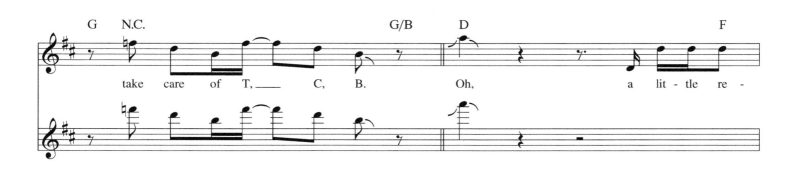

take care of T,___ C, B. Oh, a lit - tle re -

spect. Whoa___ babe, a lit - tle re - spect. Our

Shot Gun

Words and Music by Autry DeWalt

Do the jerk now. ___

Put on ___ your red dress

and then you go down - town, now.

I said to

Guitar:

mf

buy your-self a shot-gun, now.

We gon - na break it down, ba - by, now.

We're gon - na load it up, ba - by, now. ___

Ah, then you

shoot him 'fore he run, now.

I said, shot - gun. _____

Organ:

Shoot him 'fore he run, now.

Do the jerk, ba - by. ___   Do the jerk, now. ___

Hey!   Bb7

Sax solo:

Fl. ___

I said,

Bb7

shot - gun. ___   *Organ:*   Shoot him 'fore he run, now.

Do the jerk, ba - by.

Do the jerk now. Hey! Put on your high-heeled shoes.

Guitar:

I said we're go-in' down here an' lis-ten to 'em play

the blues. We're gon-na dig po-ta-ta. we're gon-na

Organ:

pick to-ma-tas I said shot-gun.

Shoot him 'fore he run, now.

Do the jerk, ba - by. ___ Do the jerk, now. ___

Hey! I said it's twin - in' time. ___ I said it's

twin - in' time. I said it's twin - in' time. Hey,

what did I say? *Sax solo:*

Fadeout

Soul Finger

Words and Music by Ben Cauley, Carl Cunningham, James Alexander,
Jimmy King, Phalon Jones and Ronnie Caldwell

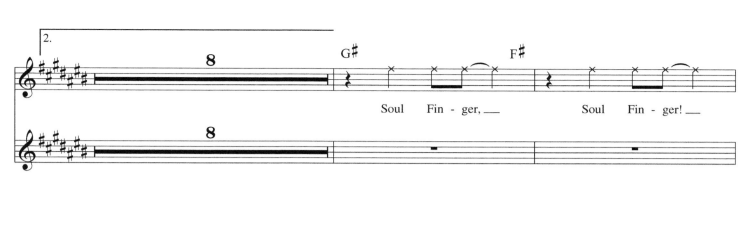

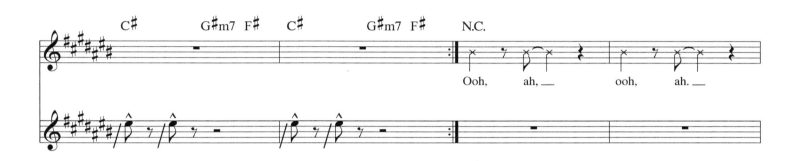

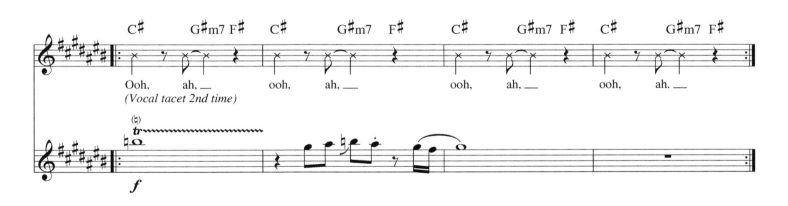

Repeat and Fade

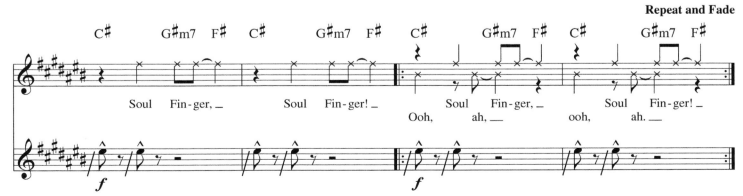

Soul Serenade

Words and Music by Curtis Ousley and Luther Dixon

Unchain My Heart

Words and Music by Bobby Sharp and Teddy Powell

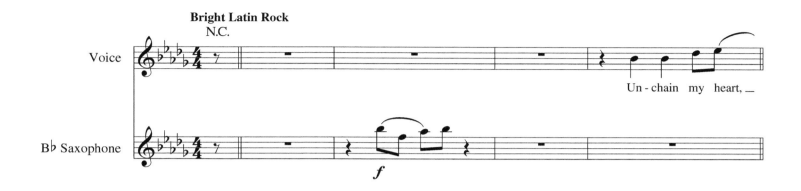

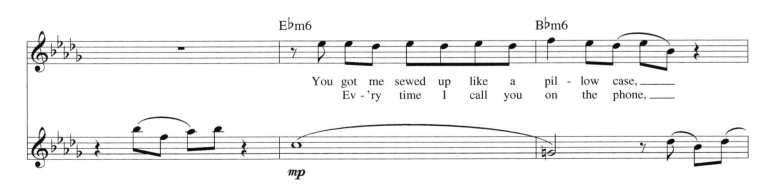

I'm un-der your spell ____ like a man in a trance. __ Oo-

whoa, ____ you know darn_ well ____ that I don't stand a chance, _

so un-chain my heart. ____ Let me go my way. ____

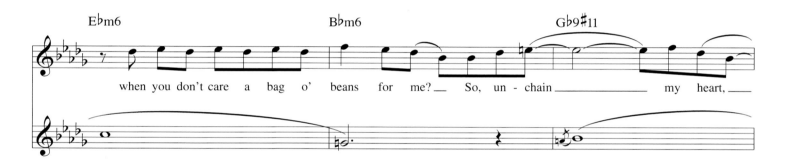

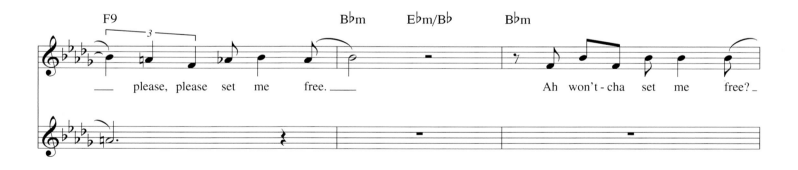

SEQUENTIAL
PIANO SONGBOOK SERIES

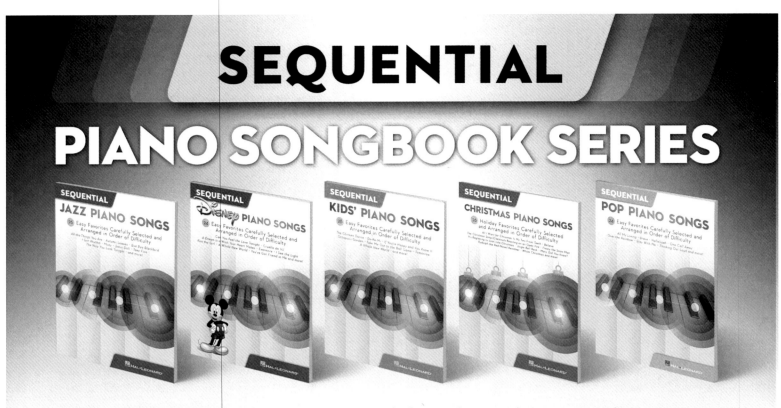

Pianists of all levels can enjoy current and classic hits with Sequential Piano Songs! Starting with the easiest arrangements (hands alone, very simple rhythms) and progressing in order of difficulty (hands together, syncopated rhythms and moving around the keyboard), these supplemental songbooks are a terrific resource for improving music reading and piano skills from the very first page.

SEQUENTIAL CHRISTMAS PIANO SONGS
26 Holiday Favorites Carefully Selected and Arranged in Order of Difficulty

All I Want for Christmas Is My Two Front Teeth • Believe • The Christmas Song (Chestnuts Roasting on an Open Fire) • Frosty the Snow Man • It's Beginning to Look like Christmas • Jingle Bell Rock • Mary, Did You Know? • Rudolph the Red-Nosed Reindeer • White Christmas • and more.

00294929 Easy Piano...$16.99

SEQUENTIAL DISNEY PIANO SONGS
24 Easy Favorites Carefully Selected and Arranged in Order of Difficulty

Be Our Guest • Can You Feel the Love Tonight • Chim Chim Cher-ee • A Dream Is a Wish Your Heart Makes • Evermore • I See the Light • Kiss the Girl • Let It Go • A Whole New World (Aladdin's Theme) • The World Es Mi Familia • You've Got a Friend in Me • and more.

00294870 Easy Piano...$16.99

SEQUENTIAL JAZZ PIANO SONGS
26 Easy Favorites Carefully Selected and Arranged in Order of Difficulty

All the Things You Are • Autumn Leaves • Bye Bye Blackbird • Fly Me to the Moon (In Other Words) • I Got Rhythm • It Could Happen to You • Misty • My Funny Valentine • Satin Doll • Stardust • Take Five • The Way You Look Tonight • When I Fall in Love • and more.

00286967 Easy Piano...$16.99

SEQUENTIAL KIDS' PIANO SONGS
24 Easy Favorites Carefully Selected and Arranged in Order of Difficulty

Best Day of My Life • Can You Feel the Love Tonight • The Chicken Dance • Do-Re-Mi • Happy Birthday to You • If You're Happy and You Know It • Let It Go • Sing • Star Wars (Main Theme) • Take Me Out to the Ball Game • This Land Is Your Land • Tomorrow • A Whole New World • and more.

00286602 Easy Piano...$16.99

SEQUENTIAL POP PIANO SONGS
24 Easy Favorites Carefully Selected and Arranged in Order of Difficulty

All My Loving • Beauty and the Beast • Brave • Daydream Believer • Feel It Still • Hallelujah • Love Me Tender • One Call Away • Over the Rainbow • Perfect • Rolling in the Deep • Shake It Off • Stay with Me • Thinking Out Loud • Unchained Melody • and more.

00279889 Easy Piano...$16.99

Disney Characters and Artwork TM & © 2019 Disney
Prices, contents, and availability subject to change without notice.

HAL•LEONARD®
www.halleonard.com